Su̲rviving Adolescents

Dr Michael Carr-Gregg is one of Australia's leading authorities on teenage behaviour, and as a practising psychologist specialises in the area of parenting adolescents and adolescent mental health.

He was founder of the world's first national support group for teenage cancer patients, CanTeen (The Australian Teenage Cancer Patient's Society). He is the consultant psychologist to many schools and national organisations, an official ambassador for the federal government's youth suicide prevention programs beyondblue and Mindmatters, and from 2005 will be the resident psychologist with Channel Nine's *Today Show*. He has written two books on parenting adolescents and is a columnist for *Girlfriend* and *Australian Doctor* magazines. He has won many awards for his work.

Surviving
Adolescents

The must-have
manual for
all parents

Dr Michael Carr-Gregg

Illustrations by Ron Tandberg

To my son Rupert

PENGUIN BOOKS

Published by the Penguin Group
Penguin Group (Australia)
250 Camberwell Road, Camberwe[ll]
(a division of Pearson Australia Gr[oup]
Penguin Group (NZ)
67 Apollo Drive, Rosedale, North
(a division of Pearson New Zealan[d]
Penguin Books (South Africa) (Pty)
24 Sturdee Avenue, Rosebank, Joh[annesburg]

Penguin Books Ltd, Registered Of[fice]

First published by Penguin Group [(Australia), 2005]

10 9 8 7 6

Text copyright © Michael Carr-Gregg, 2005
Illustrations copyright © Ron Tandberg, 2005

The moral right of the author has been asserted

Cover and text design by Jay Ryves, © Penguin Group (Australia)
Cover photograph by Yannick Fagot/photolibrary.com
Typeset in11/18 pt Simoncini Garamond by Post Pre-press Group, Brisbane, Queensland
Printed and bound in Australia by McPherson's Printing Group Pty Ltd, Maryborough, Victoria

National Library of Australia
Cataloguing-in-Publication data:

Carr-Gregg, Michael.
    Surviving adolescents: a must-have manual for all parents.

    Includes index.
    ISBN 978 0 14 300378 6.

    1. Adolescence. 2. Adolescent psychology. 3. Parent and teenager. I. Tandberg, Ron, 1943– . II. Title.

305.235

www.penguin.com.au

Foreword

Based on twenty years of research and his experience in helping hundreds of families, award-winning psychologist Dr Michael Carr-Gregg has written a powerful, practical book on how parents can manage their offspring's transition from childhood to young adulthood. With the gifts of simplicity and clarity Michael offers a range of skills, knowledge and strategies that will lighten the load for parents of today's teenagers. This book is an easy read, but its message is fresh, nuanced and important. You'll finish it feeling as if you've just had a cuppa with someone who is not only entertaining and enlightening but knows exactly how it feels to be the parent of a twenty-first-century teen. If I had a magic wand, I would give this book to every parent. It is indeed a must-read!

Steve Vizard AO

Contents

Introduction: be alert but not alarmed!

Of all the natural events that occur in the family life-cycle, the emergence of adolescence is the one most likely to test parental flexibility and tolerance. Twenty-first-century parents require a new set of skills, knowledge and strategies to cope with the upheaval that is the changing face of adolescence. Research suggests that one in five families across the western world has one child at home whose behaviour is so difficult that it is hard for them to lead a normal life.

The last Australian Bureau of Statistics census estimated that by 2005 there would be some 4.6 million 12–17-year-olds in Australia. Their research also suggests that most of them (almost 80 per cent) will get through adolescence without any major developmental disruption or 'wardrobe malfunction'. But it must be said that many will treat their pet cactus better than their parents during this time, with raised voices, slammed doors and tectonic tantrums being the order of the day.

Research studies from around the world say that one of the most important factors in the lives of young people is a close relationship with an adult. Most parents, I know, struggle to generate the psychological sinew required, are time-poor and often don't have the energy or even the inclination to attend information sessions on freezing evenings, let alone read a weighty treatise on developmental psychology. So in this book I have set out to

provide a concise guide to surviving daily life with adolescents. I'm a great believer in trying to keep advice to parents as realistic and practical as possible. For this reason, as well as suggesting some strategic approaches, I have also included wherever possible what may seem to some of you to be fairly basic tips. These may seem obvious, but I know from personal and professional experience that they are things it's all too easy to forget in the heat of battle. After all, forewarned is forearmed!

Although raising young people can be full of challenges, especially when they seem constantly to make decisions that fly in the face of common sense, there are few things in this world more satisfying than surveying the final product. Despite the developmental challenges adolescents face, many demonstrate formidable grit and determination and end up making us all immensely proud.

Michael Carr-Gregg, 2005

The rocky road that is adolescence

The word 'adolescence' comes from the Latin *adolescere,* which means to grow to maturity. Adolescents are in a unique developmental phase, a period of transition with a succession of (perfectly normal!) physical, psychological and emotional changes. They are no longer children, nor are they yet adults, and therein lies the root of their problems. They are striving for independence and autonomy, yet are still fragile beings in the process of growing and developing.

> **'You don't have to be a poet to suffer.
> Adolescence is enough suffering for anyone.'**
> John Ciardi

In childhood, growth is slow and steady; at puberty, change is rapid and dramatic as hormones start cascading through the body. Adolescents can experience dramatic growth spurts, some growing up to 10 centimetres in a year and gaining 9–13 kilos. Sadly, not all parts of the body grow and develop at the same time or rate – the hands and feet typically grow faster than the arms and legs, as a result of which adolescents may often be un-coordinated (so, be tolerant if food or drinks are spilt). Around one in five adolescents experience growing pains (usually briefly and at night), typically in the form of aches in the shins, calves or thighs.

Adolescence ain't what it used to be . . .

As you may already have noticed, young people now enter puberty earlier than ever before and leave home later. The Aus-tralian Medical Association now defines adolescents as those

between ages 10 and 24, whereas once the term mainly referred to teenagers. The average age at which young women have their first period is now 12, rather than 16 as was the case a century ago. And note that this is the average: a 2000 UK study of 14 000 children found that one in six girls now reach puberty by 8 years of age, compared to one in 100 a generation ago.

No one really knows why this is happening, though better nutrition, oestrogen in hair products, chemicals in the environment, high rates of obesity, and the presence of growth hormones in the food chain have all been suggested as possible factors. Recent research from New Zealand indicates that one of the most important factors in early female puberty may be the quality of a father's investment in the family: put simply, good relationships lead to later puberty. However, the same study suggests that there is a direct correlation between the absence of a father and early onset of menstruation and the incidence of teenage pregnancy. The presence of a stepfather, somewhat spookily, appears to correlate with earlier puberty in girls living away from their biological father, so with more single parents re-partnering we are likely to see even more young people hitting puberty earlier.)

The three faces of adolescents

Adolescence involves three distinct phases: early (Am I normal?), middle (Who am I?) and late (Where am I going?).

Early adolescents undergo many physical, emotional and mental changes that together can throw their lives and those of their parents off-balance. These young people can become very self-conscious and are often overly sensitive about themselves, worrying about personal qualities or 'defects' that loom large for them but are hardly noticeable to others. They may even begin to question whether they are actually normal.

It is around this time that the quiet, compliant child of recent memory suddenly changes. A voice from within tells the young person to turn away from childhood and childish things, and from their parents. This breaking of emotional bonds with parents is aided by changes in the brain that enable the adolescent to develop more adult thought processes. It is as if a veil lifts and they see their parents for the very first time, through new eyes. And their reaction is very often 'Oh my God, what have I got for parents!'

> **'The four stages of life are infancy, childhood, adolescence, and obsolescence.'**
> Art Linklater

Having come face to face for the first time with the terrible flaws in their parents, *middle adolescents* develop a fierce interest in, and seek comfort among, their peers. Middle adolescents surround themselves with the myriad symbols of their generation – the music, the clothes, the piercings and the tatts, the hairstyles. They seek to establish their own identity and individuality by spurning adult control and support. Relationships with parents can become significantly strained at this time, but happily this usually only lasts for a relatively short time. The paradox is that even though they appear to be pushing us away, in truth middle adolescents need a guide who can nourish their uniqueness. So keep the lines of communication open!

By *late adolescence* most young people have come to terms with their identity and have begun to define and understand their role in life. Their relationships with adults change and are based more on mutual respect and affection, as they realise that

'The young always have the same problem –
how to rebel and conform at the same time.
They have now solved this by defying their parents
and copying one another.'

Quentin Crisp

compared to others their parents aren't that bad after all! Late adolescents tend to be more committed and responsible, and some begin focusing on (even planning for) the future. But they still need, and are more accepting of, an adult in their life, to help them set goals and develop strategies to achieve these.

How the teenage brain differs from an adult's

Our brain is only fully formed when we're in our early twenties. While an adolescent's capacity for gut reactions is wired in, their ability to discern, handle ambiguous information, coordinate conflicting signals, plan, organise, or control their emotions is still under construction. Adolescents can watch multiple

screens simultaneously and listen to music at the same time, but they cannot keep track of multiple thoughts and cannot recall past experiences instantly in order to factor them into a present decision. For this reason they may also have trouble organising several tasks (for example, which to do first: call a friend, wash the dishes, or do the assignment that's due in the morning?).

Most importantly, while adults use the critical-thinking part of the brain to assess risk, teenagers considering risky behaviours (sex, drugs, driving cars, etc.) use the more primitive, instinctual part of the brain (known as the amygdala). This is probably why young people so often get it wrong: on the one hand they lack experience and on the other their brain wiring is incomplete. This in turn is why we need to set limits and boundaries, especially when it comes to issues related to safety.

A testing time for all

In short, in making the journey between childhood and young adulthood, adolescents are faced with four main challenges: forming a positive identity; establishing a set of good friends; breaking the emotional bonds that bound them to their adult carers; and setting meaningful vocational goals. Not all will tackle these tasks during adolescence – some young people take longer than others to gain the traction to find themselves.

At the same time, adolescence is characterised by:

- a belief in one's immortality
- a desire to experiment
- a need for peer approval
- relatively short-term relationships.

So while developmental changes can in themselves be testing for parents, perhaps our greatest fear is that these may lead to risky behaviours that may compromise their health.

The good news is that today's teens are not impossible to deal with, especially if you apply the knowledge, skill and strategies in this book!

> '**I never expected to see the day**
> **when girls would get sunburned**
> **in the places they do now.**'
> Will Rogers

What enables young people to flourish?

Psychologists over the years have looked at young people from disadvantaged backgrounds and found that resilient young people share five key traits.

1 **Having an adult mentor or role model in their lives**

One of the best forms of insurance for the physical and emotional wellbeing of young people is to have in their lives just one special adult from whom they can draw strength, who

makes them feel safe, valued and listened to. This doesn't have to be a parent: it could be an uncle, teacher, friend of the family, coach or grandparent. If young people have a special bond that they value highly, they are more likely to think twice before doing anything to damage the connection. Building this 'connectedness' with your adolescent maximises your chance of successful parenting. This is good news for single parents, who often report feeling less than adequate.

2 **Having something they're good at**
Providing young people with a succession of structured activities they are good at and enjoy (art, music, sport, dance, drama), and for which they receive recognition, is very valuable. It allows them to mix with peers who share similar interests or values, exposes them to good adult role models, and imposes routine on their lives.

3 **Having emotional intelligence**
Another crucial advantage in navigating adolescence is the ability to read social situations – to name and recognise the thoughts and emotions of others, and to see how one is coming across to other people. These skills can be learnt by example, or be taught.

4 **Having a sense of meaning in their lives**

It is important for young people to feel connected to something or someone that transcends the material world in which we live. Almost everyone who's studied adolescents and spirituality has found it to be a protective factor: by buffering the impact of life stresses it can make it less likely that they will resort to smoking, drinking and using illicit drugs.

5 **Positive self-talk and a willingness to persevere**

Self-talk is our thoughts making themselves known to us and it influences our self-esteem and confidence, positively or negatively. If adolescents tell themselves they are a failure, they will be. If they tell themselves they can succeed, they have a much greater chance of doing so. Resilient teenagers talk encouragingly to themselves, and it's important that we reinforce this with positive messages.

'Adolescents are not monsters.
They are just people trying to learn
how to make it among the adults in the world,
who are probably not so sure themselves.'

Virginia Satir

Knowing your parenting script

While their ultimate goal is to achieve freedom and they will do all they can to attain it, teenagers still need to feel their parents' strength and love. Even those who seem to be fighting tooth and nail to dismantle our authority know deep-down that they would be well and truly undone if they were too successful. The more young people feel themselves on their own and without parental support, the more vulnerable they are. So great parenting is about striking a balance between being an army sergeant and a Mother Teresa.

> **'There is no such thing**
> **as a perfect parent.'**
> John Cheetham

Every adult has a parenting script which they learnt when *they* were being brought up. It's like a built-in microchip programmed while we were children: it often governs how we parent our own kids and can lower the IQ even of an intellectual giant.

Adolescent psychologists have long been interested in how parents influence the development of teens. One of the most robust approaches is the study of what has been called 'parenting style'. *Responsive* parents intentionally foster their children's individuality, self-regulation and self-assertion, by being supportive and attuned to their special needs and demands. *Demanding* parents prefer behavioural control, expecting their teens to be mature and play a constructive part in family life, at the same time supervising them and being willing to confront and discipline

YOUR MOTHER AND I HAVE BOUGHT A LITTLE BOOK WHICH WILL HELP US UNDERSTAND YOU

IT'S THE SAME SIZE AS YOUR WALLET

disobedient offspring. Between these two extremes there are three main parenting styles:

- **authoritarian: limits set, but not negotiated**
  Such parents are highly demanding and directive, but not responsive. They seek obedience and expect their orders to be obeyed without explanation. These parents provide a well-ordered and structured environment with clearly stated rules.
- **authoritative: limits set, but negotiated**
  These parents are both demanding and responsive. They monitor and impart clear standards for their teenager's conduct. They are firm but not intrusive or restrictive; their disciplinary methods are supportive, rather than punitive. They want their children to be assertive as well as socially responsible, self-regulated as well as cooperative.
- **'Woodstock' model: no limits or boundaries**
  These are indulgent parents stuck in the sixties – more responsive than demanding. They do not require their

offspring to behave maturely; they allow considerable self-regulation and avoid confrontation – all conducive to full-tilt indolence in young people.

> **'Adolescence – a brief period of optimism,**
> **separating a brief period of ignorance**
> **from a terminal period of cynicism.'**
> Philip Adams

Get (and stay) involved in their life

Several studies have suggested that young people who are 'connected' and involved with their families are less prone to violence, drug and alcohol abuse, and low self-esteem than those who lead increasingly separate lives. So try to eat in as often as possible, sit down for dinner with them at least once a week (and use the time to talk – don't eat in front of the TV), share as many activities as possible, and make sure your work-hours don't keep you away from home. And be careful not to overuse electronic babysitters (TV, internet, video games and so on) that may keep them busy but are no substitute for human interaction. Your offspring needs your personal attention, even if they often may not act as if they do! They will remember the rituals and traditions you create.

Possible activities

Most teens, naturally enough, would prefer to be with their mates than hang out with their parents. Nonetheless, there will always be opportunities for you to spend time together – especially when their own plans fall through. When this chance arises, seize the day!

Whatever activity you share, it must be something they enjoy – engaging them in activities of your choice is counter-productive and reduces the likelihood that they'll come back for a second dose. Some ideas:

- Ask them to make a family movie. They could then download it onto a computer, edit it and choose a soundtrack.
- Take them to (and stay to watch) any sport or other activity (drama, music) they're involved in.
- Take (don't just send) them to a concert. They get to pick the music, and you resist the urge to complain about it.
- Do something useful in the community. Volunteer at a homeless shelter or local children's hospital, or do some work for a cause they support.
- Listen. Set aside time on a semi-regular basis and let them know you're available to listen to anything they have to say on any topic at all. Give advice only if they ask for it.

- Do something familiar. It's not just toddlers who love repetition – rituals and routines are comforting for everyone and they help shape a family's identity.
- Best of all, spend a completely unstructured day with your adolescent, doing exactly what they want to do. Ignore the phone, emails, work and errands, and focus completely on them. Top off the day with an ice-cream sundae.

Whatever you do, make sure that you touch your teenager (lie down together at bedtime, give a relaxed hair-brushing, have a wrestling match, or spend a half-hour together on the couch in front of TV). No one needs to remind parents to cuddle their infants, but like bedtime stories hugging can go by the wayside during adolescence, which is a pity. It's amazing how many teens are 'skin-hungry'.

Set limits

One of the keys to parenting adolescents is making sure they feel safe. This can be communicated through the establishment, early in adolescence, of rules that are agreed by both sides. There is no point in drawing lines in the sand and expecting young people to 'obey': adolescents are programmed not to. The smart money is on parents who create a negotiated system of rewards and punishments, which gives adolescents the feeling that they have some ownership of the rules.

Be sure to set very clear boundaries, which communicates to your offspring that you care. Don't forget that he or she is a 'work in progress' and can be greatly helped by having explicit guidelines. Too many parents today are hesitant to set limits, instead creating a culture of entitlement (all rights, no responsibilities) which can create lifelong problems.

A word of caution, though. When young people are *too* constrained their world can seem very negative, which is just about guaranteed to engender rebellion and clashes. As parents, our job is to choose carefully and find a balance between too many and too few boundaries. One example might be negotiating a curfew: ask them what they consider a reasonable hour to be home, agree on a time and then in the same way establish what the consequences will be if the agreed time is not met. Once your adolescent seems ready to take on (safely) more responsibility, these rules should be revisited. A curfew might, for example, be re-negotiated every few months, with a view to allowing a later time. Even where boundaries are in place, trust and respect are the operative words.

> **'Teenagers complain there's nothing to do,**
> **then stay out all night doing it.'**
> Bob Phillips

Teach them consequential learning

One consequence is worth a thousand words, a fact that can be an important tool for changing adolescent behaviour and instilling responsibility. Teaching young people the principles of cause and effect helps them accept 'ownership' of their actions. It prepares them for life in the real world.

The traditional reward-and-punishment method of discipline is not helpful, as it impedes adolescents from making decisions and taking responsibility for them. It is important that they learn by experience the benefits of appropriate behaviour and the disadvantages of inappropriate behaviour, especially if safety is a factor.

And the consequence was . . .

This approach has all sorts of applications in everyday life. If, for instance, your offspring has accepted responsibility for one or more tasks around the house (taking out the rubbish, washing dishes, mowing the lawn, babysitting younger children, etc.), it

is essential to negotiate the consequences of not fulfilling their obligations. Without consequences there is no structure, no teaching or learning of responsibility, and discipline problems start to crop up.

That said, it's a good idea to wean your teen on low-risk consequences first, working up to the heavy stuff. Realistic consequences have the greatest impact. If your adolescent has trouble getting out of bed, don't play them your old John Denver records at full volume or invite their friends over to breakfast in their room. Just let them pay the price if they don't get up.

Remember, time is as tight as a tourniquet. Consequences should be imposed as soon after the infringement as possible.

Some suggestions for effective consequences:
• Restrictions on socialising ('grounding', as it is commonly called) for a brief period of time.

- Removal of privileges (TV, internet, video games or mobile phone) for a brief period of time.
- Withholding of some or all pocket money, whether or not it is usually received for work done.

If your offspring continually fails to do agreed tasks, the negotiated consequence should be applied consistently. Depending on the behaviour (e.g. breaking a curfew), it may be appropriate to increase the consequence. If a brief war of attrition over two or three weeks brings no behaviour change, it is possible that something else may be behind it and it would be wise to seek professional help.

What to do when you're desperate!

Desperate times sometimes call for desperate measures. One family sought my help because their chronically slothful teens were forever leaving their belongings around the house. The parents were sick and tired of picking up after them, but they'd tried everything – threats, rewards, yelling. I suggested a family meeting where the parents were to propose a new protocol (no more raised voices) and a simple plan whereby any belongings left lying around in the public areas of the house would simply be placed in the deep-freezer in the garage. There would be nothing said: that's where their things would be. After a few weeks of frozen socks and undies, the message was well and truly received. (For more on this trying topic, see 'Getting help around the house' on page 69).

> 'Before I got married,
> I had six theories about bringing up children.
> Now I have six children and no theories.'
> Earl of Rochester

Give them your trust and respect

The best relationships between teenagers and their parents are based on trust and respect. But many parents instead find themselves floundering in a sea of desperation and anxiety. Ideally, trust and respect grow incrementally as rules and regulations are negotiated. In this way the young person comes to associate compliance with the possibility of having rules re-negotiated in their favour as they demonstrate their trustworthiness. If parents are consistent and follow through with rewards and punishments, the young person will tend to respond in kind. If, on the other hand, you change the rules and fail to keep promises, the young person will run like a Sherman tank through the framework you have attempted to set up.

A note for fathers

Having spent years talking to young people about their parents, it's clear to me that young people, especially boys, get a lot out of being around their fathers – something special and complementary to what their mothers give them. Great fathering is not about being seen as a walking wallet, rather it is about spending quantity time with your kids, especially in early adolescence. Most Aussie kids aren't big on Brady-Bunch-type 'deep and meaningfuls'. In Anglo-Saxon countries such as Australia and the UK, talking and listening tend to occur amidst activity, with trust and self-disclosure growing

HE HASN'T HAD TIME TO TELL YOU, BUT YOUR FATHER'S WORRIED YOU'LL AMOUNT TO NOTHING

gradually as a result. So doing stuff together is vital – it allows closeness and it allows conversation to wander into deeper realms. Being your offspring's taxi-driver is a good opportunity. And see if you can find common interests (perhaps a sport, or a game like chess): boys in particular will open up more while doing things.

Top tips for youth-friendly communication

1 Talk less and listen more

Young people's most common complaint is that their parents don't give them a fair hearing. When young people speak, make sure they know you are listening: put down the paper, turn off the TV, and look at them. Listen carefully without interrupting and then feed back to them what they have said. This tells them not only that you heard but also that you took it in.

2 Keep it short

When you do speak, don't go on and on. This is supposed to be
a dialogue, not an oration. Research says that the average teenager has an attention span of about 13.6 seconds for what their
parents have to say. So if you haven't said anything important by
then, you are in trouble . . .

> '**There's nothing wrong with today's teenager**
> **that twenty years won't cure.**'
>
> Anon.

3 Use humour

US president Franklin D. Roosevelt once observed that the saving grace of American families was the fact that the overwhelming majority were possessed of two great qualities – a sense of humour and a sense of proportion. Many parents (especially dads) use what they think is humour, but it is too often in the form of put-downs and sarcasm, which actually triggers a defensive response and shuts the communication door they are trying to keep open. Given that many young people complain their parents are too serious, need to lighten up and take a 'chill pill', the appropriate use of humour is a great way to improve communication. The rules are simple: keep it upbeat and make sure that you are funny (if you're not sure, check with a partner or friend!).

4 Avoid issuing ultimatums

Try not to use language that triggers an adolescent's inherent sensitivity to control matters. If you issue an ultimatum, either they will take up your challenge (and so you have doubled your

trouble!) or you will have to back down and you lose credibility. The trick is to think ahead and ask yourself whether you can find a compromise solution where everyone wins a little.

> 'The face of a child can say it all,
> especially the mouth part of the face.'
>
> Jack Handy

5   Be your kid's greatest fan

Regularly give positive feedback. Research suggests that Australian teenagers, when in conversation with their parents, generally get only one positive message (e.g. 'Hey, you did that really well') for every five negative ones ('You got 75% in your maths test? What happened to the other 25%?'). Compliment them as often as possible on all their efforts, on the strength of their character and on their individuality. Try to catch your adolescent doing something good, and send a positive message – make it a goal to say at least one constructive thing a day.

They may do little more than grunt, shrug and slope off to their room, but it's all about putting a penny in the bank of goodwill for later on.

6 Don't constantly remind them of past mistakes

Apart from the fact that adolescence is a time of trial and error when mistakes are expected, constantly reminding a teen of past goofs (especially if you do so with apparent relish) makes

it less likely that they'll tell you next time they stuff up. And their lasting memory will be of parental monologues laced with constant backbiting.

7 Talk while doing something together

For some parents, catching up comes naturally around the dinner table or before bedtime. But one of the greatest inventions for parents of teenagers was the car. This is because when you are driving your offspring somewhere, especially to a destination of their choice (a friend's place, a concert, a sporting event), they can't escape. This is a brilliant opportunity to engage them in conversation – nothing too heavy, just a low-key 'How are things going?' kind of exchange, even just to find out one important thing about your teen's day. It is a way of letting them know you are interested in them, their life and their point of view. You'll find that boys in particular are much more likely to talk if you are kicking a ball around with them.

8 Let some things go by you

One of the most annoying things that we parents can do is comment on everything our adolescent says or does. Imagine if you had someone constantly remarking on your actions throughout the day – it would drive you nuts. Parents who keep up a running commentary dramatically reduce the likelihood of receiving any information in future. Young people don't respond well to being constantly offered an editorial on their lives.

Life wasn't meant to be easy

As described earlier, adolescence can be a frightening and troublesome time. The basically small, safe, secure world of the child suddenly metamorphoses into the large, unfamiliar world of the near-adult. Life will inevitably involve some emotional ups and downs as both adolescent and parents strive to cope with these dramatic changes. If we don't allow adolescents some autonomy they will rebel, because they'll feel deprived of choice and the opportunity to make mistakes – from which they can learn.

Few parents want their offspring hanging around, dependent and unable to make a decision, at 30 years of age. It is normal as well as necessary that young people gradually drift away from us. So, let go. Start when they are in middle adolescence by giving up the unequal struggle against the trivial things such as peer-led hairstyles, music, clothing and behaviours that annoy, embarrass or offend you or other adults. Be prepared for adolescents to depart from your value system as they experiment and eventually find their own place in the world.

> '**The young are always ready to give,**
> **to those who are older than themselves,**
> **the full benefit of their inexperience.**'
>
> Oscar Wilde

Girls, girls, girls

There is a consensus among many parents that teenage girls require more work and 'higher maintenance' than boys. Irrespective of

social class, parents' tales of their teenage daughters are frequently delivered with eye rollings and sighs. Parents see girls as more multifaceted, more complex emotionally, more manipulative and infinitely more moody than boys.

The primary reason for this is the issue of separation. Most normal adolescents at some time find it totally unacceptable to be dependent on their parents, particularly their mother. But, unlike boys, teenage girls tend not to withdraw but instead to engage in an unrelenting 'shock and awe' battle with their parents, again particularly their mother. This can test even the most resilient and understanding parent.

Culture clash

For years now, I have had the privilege of sitting in my consulting rooms and witnessing some of the most savage psychological battles imaginable, almost always between teenage girls and their mothers. While I have not read this in any manual of adolescent psychology, it seems to me that is most often with teenage girls that parents experience the extreme disturbance of adolescence, as their innocent, loving, poetry-writing darling morphs into a distant, defiant, sexually aware stranger.

Why do they do this? Simple. Young women solve the problem of being around their parents and dealing with their unacceptable feelings of love and dependence by waging war on everything and everyone. Life becomes a fight. Adolescent girls,

being more emotionally sophisticated and ten times more verbal than their male counterparts, will frequently target their mother and press her most sensitive buttons over and over again.

Experience suggests that some teenage girls maintain a warm relationship with their father, assuming that Dad has not beat a hasty retreat to the world of pub, work or football club, communicates in a youth-friendly way and is prepared to negotiate. Yet, with few exceptions, an adolescent girl's attachment to her mother is stronger than to her father, which means that much more negativism is required to deny the strength of that bond.

The situation is compounded by the fact that teenage girls argue far more than boys do, having already had practice within their peer group in pre-adolescence. Relationships between girls at this age can be verbally nasty, and they are far better equipped than boys to deal with the emotional and tear-stained exchanges that characterise their relationships with their parents.

Top 5 tactics

If you have a daughter who is physically well developed but still emotionally immature, consider some of the following strategies.

1 Give serious thought to a single-sex school

This will allow her to 'grow' at her own pace in an environment where gender stereotypes are less of a major factor. Single-sex education helps channel sensation-seekers into healthy risks through sports like netball, hockey and soccer, which they can play with gusto without worrying about appearing like tomboys. In addition, my experience is that staff at single-sex schools have a great understanding of how girls learn, and tend to adapt their teaching styles accordingly.

2 Actively model your value system

Teach your girl assertive communication, conflict resolution and anger management by example.

3 **Help her build self-confidence**

Encourage her to set goals, praise her when she's succeeded, and then set more. Self-confidence will increase her ability to negotiate the social minefield that is teenage girlhood, and resist peer pressure to take unhealthy risks.

4 **Consequential learning is a beautiful thing.**

Make sure your daughter is answerable when being nasty: explain the consequences if she spreads gossip, and let her know from an early age that she is responsible for what she creates in her life.

5 **Teach her to treat others with respect**

Almost all teenagers want to 'belong' and be accepted. Reassure your daughter that she is under no obligation to be everybody's friend, that treating everyone with respect will make her less likely to be a victim of bullying.

About a boy

Boys, by contrast, are viewed by parents, with few exceptions, as more straightforward and even-tempered, easier to read and far less judgemental than girls. At the same time, parents often ask why it is that boys share so few of their emotions and, generally speaking, express less emotion. The answer is that they actually experience fewer emotions than their female counterparts: they don't have as many neural pathways between the emotion

DARLING... YOUR DINNER'S
GETTING COLD .... MUM

centres and the verbal centres, and they have fewer verbal centres in the brain. In short, they generally don't produce as many words and so don't have as many words to fit their emotions. In addition, many boys are systematically steered away from their emotional selves during middle and late childhood.

> 'A boy becomes an adult three years before
> his parents think he does,
> and about two years after he thinks he does.'
> Lewis B. Hershey

How you can help

So what can you do? Some suggestions:

- **Teach them how to manage their anger**
  Many boys seem to have just two switches – 'off' and 'rage'. Their emotions are often channelled through anger, as this is commonly the only acceptable response within the peer

group. Giving boys words for the hurt, anxiety, frustration, disappointment and shame means they can begin to deal with it, and help themselves.

- **Use praise and rewards**
  Boys seek and respond to immediate praise and rewards. So make every effort to praise yours when he has done something laudable.

Body art and other questionable fashions

Since ancient times, parent-offending clothing, hairstyles and body art (heavy-metal inserts, for instance, or 'tribal' tatts) have all been part of teenagers' attempts to find an identity and to express their individuality and independence.

Warning, warning, Will Robinson! This is a horror zone that requires dextrous handling if you want a reasonable quality of life. If you constantly focus on these manifestations, rather than simply expressing disapproval once and letting things work

YOUR FATHER'S NOT HAPPY

themselves out, your young person may end up rebelling even more and a power struggle is likely to follow.

So try tapping into your sense of optimism (no doubt long dormant) and awareness, and save your energy for bigger issues. In other words, if they turn up on your doorstep with hair the colour of exotic Peruvian butterflies try to resist the temptation to ask what time the Mardi Gras begins – instead bite your tongue and bury your head in the newspaper.

School

Research says a lot of things about school (much of it less than helpful) but credible boffins suggest that one of the greatest predictors of success in life is literacy in Year 9. The research is also crystal-clear that one of the most important predictors of whether they'll be able to read or write is the relationship they have with their teacher.

Students will work for teachers that they love, and we parents have an important role in encouraging our offspring to develop good relationships with their teachers. If a teenager repeatedly complains about hating school, it is your job to find out why and to offer to help. Make sure they know that you care about their happiness, take their concerns seriously and want to work towards a resolution. If a young person is persistently unhappy at school, and it's not just negative feng shui, consider alternative schools, home schooling, TAFE or letting them take a year off for travel or a part-time job.

There is often too much hype about the final years of school and we need to keep this in perspective. The final year is, of course, important in their lives, but it is not the be-all-and-end-all. It is just another stage in a student's career, and the sun and the moon and the stars do not revolve around what happens at the end of it. Senior students should not embark on some kind of monastic existence: the secret of success at this time is sleep, equilibrium and routine. The research is again clear that students who succeed are focused, disciplined and work hard but manage to maintain a nice balance between work and play. Getting enough sleep, relaxation and exercise, eating sensibly and drinking enough H_2O all help maintain motivation. School should end with a bang, not a whimper!

And bear in mind that studying is made much easier if young people have a goal to work towards, are sure that they want to be at school and have chosen the right subjects (i.e. ones that they enjoy and are even passionate about). As the Roman philosopher Seneca once said, 'When a man does not know what port he is headed for, no wind is the right wind'.

Education for all?

If your adolescent is a girl, school is probably not going to be a major problem unless she has a learning difficulty or disability. Statistics tell us that girls are working harder than boys, and getting better and better results. Research from New South Wales, for example, suggests that, if this situation is allowed to continue, within a decade seven out of ten students enrolled at Sydney University would be female.

There is, though, something amiss when it comes to boys' education. For the last fifteen years, boys have been achieving at significantly lower levels than girls in all areas of the curriculum.

A BOY HANDING HIS WORK IN

Generally speaking, boys read less than girls, have an attention span like that of a goldfish when it comes to school and/or homework, and are massively overrepresented in school detentions, suspensions and expulsions.

But if documenting the nature and extent of the problem was hard, try finding a simple solution! Australian educators continue to engage in passionate debate about how to better address boys' needs at school and get them back to learning. The truth is that for many boys their schools remains a psychological wasteland where they don't feel safe, valued or listened to.

How to help boys get more out of school

While we are waiting for schools to take up the challenge of creating boy-friendly schools (like appointing a boys'-education coordinator to give the issue a profile and push some of the research recommendations), there are a few things it's worth knowing. The following tips come from a variety of educators who have spent years investigating these issues: they may help you at home, and it might even be worthwhile asking the school principal politely whether the school has considered them.

Writing is a problem area for many boys. The fluency and volume of their writing is dramatically increased when they are given the opportunity to talk things through before putting pen to paper.

Educationists suggest using fluorescent lighting less, because more subdued lighting results in more settled behaviour by boys and simultaneously creates an atmosphere in which they are more able to talk about their feelings.

Last but not least, unless we help boys feel secure, valuable and accepted in schools we will continue to see unacceptable levels of depression, anxiety and self-harm. If you believe your boy is isolated or at risk in some other way, talk to his teacher.

There is clearly much that can and should be done. Is it happening at your son's school? If not, why not ? Get up and be an advocate for your child.

Bullying

Bullying shouldn't be dismissed as a harmless schoolyard rite of passage. It is a major problem in Australian schools and has serious consequences in the short, medium and long terms. And

DO YOU HAVE A PROBLEM?

despite what you may have heard, it happens in all schools – state, Catholic and independent.

School bullying involves the psychological, emotional, social or physical harassment of one student by another (though teachers and parents can also be bullies or targets too). It may be verbal (face to face, or via phone, text or email messages), nonverbal (body language), or physical and/or antisocial (gossip, exclusion). It can vary from direct to indirect harassment, from minor irritation to major assault, from 'just having a bit of fun' to breaking the law.

Many bullies don't realise, at the conscious level, that their behaviours are abusive, but unconsciously they know they are taking away the target's power. Australian research says that one in six students are bullied weekly and bothered by it: 54 per cent of Year 7 students say they feel unsafe at school. Sadly, many believe that bullying cannot be stopped and almost half the victims tell no one that it's happened. Of those who do, most tell their friends first, then Mum then Dad, and teachers last of all. We know that boys and girls are equally involved and that bullying by girls is more subtle and psychological, involving teasing, taunting and isolation.

The reason bullying continues to occur is largely because those who observe it choose to do nothing (eight out of 10 bystanders do not intervene). There is an unwritten school commandment that 'Thou shalt not dob!', not least because most students believe that nothing can be done or that to do anything will only make matters worse. This, of course, plays directly into the hands of the bully.

How to tell if your son or daughter is being bullied

Parents have a key role to play in relation to bullying – both in recognising if their child is being bullied and in reporting it. Be vigilant for the signs, which include:

- being frightened of walking to or from school, or changing their usual route
- being unwilling to go to school at all and/or beginning to skip school
- beginning to do poorly in schoolwork
- coming home regularly with belongings damaged or destroyed
- becoming withdrawn, distressed and anxious
- crying themselves to sleep or having nightmares
- regularly 'losing' possessions, food or money
- becoming unreasonable and aggressive
- giving improbable excuses to explain any of the above.

Some dos and don'ts if your child is being bullied

- **Do** act right away. Your teenager needs you to advocate on his or her behalf.
- **Do** remember that schools have a duty of care towards their students. So as soon as possible contact the school (phone, email or seek a face-to-face meeting). If you are

unsatisfied with the results, go directly to the principal. It is also a good idea to keep a written record of all phone conversations and meetings you attend.

- **Don't** attempt to contact the bully's parents – it's not your job. Leave it to the school and take it up with the principal if they don't follow through.

- **Don't** tell them to fight back, because that can lead to much more serious harm and even accusations that *they* are the bully.

What if it's your child doing the bullying?

Should your offspring be identified as a bully, it is important to seek help in changing their behaviour. Bullying has been found to interfere with learning, friendships, work, intimate relationships, income and mental health. It may also be an outward sign of depression, so a professional assessment is a good idea.

Getting help around the house

'He's a lazy little sod, I can't get him to lift a finger around the house.' The mother sitting opposite me in my consulting-room sighed with exasperation and proceeded to tell me how much ironing, washing, vacuuming and cleaning up she was doing for her adolescent son. She'd tried everything – rosters stuck on fridge doors, reward systems, bribery (cash incentives, scratchies), various forms of punishment, screaming and yelling. Finally she had given up in despair and now did it all herself, to avoid her life becoming a carp-fest.

MUM DOES THE HOUSEWORK ... I DO THE HOMEWORK

This is a worldwide phenomenon and it's getting worse: one US study has shown that the average 12–17-year-old did six hours of housework a week in 1985, four hours in 1995 and a measly two hours in 2002. Even if one factors in the busier schedules that kids have today, with sundry sports, clubs, extracurricular activities, jobs and homework, it remains an extremely frustrating state of affairs for mums and dads. But there is a solution.

> 'There's nothing wrong with the younger generation
> that becoming taxpayers won't cure.'
>
> Dan Bennett

Getting teenagers to help around the house is, of course, easier if you start training them early: many toddlers regard these activities as a game and derive enormous satisfaction from their parents' praise while they do it. The frustrated parent wringing her hands in my room had made a fatal error. For various reasons she had not given her offspring any responsible household jobs when he was young, so he had grown up without feeling the slightest need to make any contribution to the smooth running of the household. And now her hormone-drenched offspring resented being asked to do just about anything.

So what advice did I give? Well, I started with my home-grown philosophy that anybody old enough to create a mess is old enough to clean it up! I strongly believe that kids should help around the house – namely, that our job as parents is to instil in our youngsters the skills they will need when they are adults. Doing household jobs teaches them responsibility, lets them know that no one is the family servant – after all, one day they will be on their own and have to do laundry and scrub the toilet. Most important, it spreads the load.

A five-step approach to the slothful teen syndrome

This is a simple if not quite stress-free system. Before you get started, though, I recommend you equip yourself for the fray.

First, abandon whatever approach you have been taking until now. It hasn't worked and you don't need a psychologist to tell you that if you keep doing the same thing you'll only ever get the same result. It's also vital to lose the Rambo attitude and the ultimatums. Threats are the most common and least effective parental tactic, because they automatically trigger defensiveness and a power struggle. Finally, prepare yourself psychologically for the fact that the first few weeks of the new regimen will be tedious and a burden. Just try to keep in mind that you are going through this in order to give your adolescent both a sense of responsibility and a work ethic.

Letting them have fun while they work is likely to encourage cooperation. They could, for example, play their favourite music, nice and loud throughout the house, while they're doing the vacuuming.

So, down to business.

1 Start by drawing up a list of regular, age-appropriate jobs that need to be done. Make sure the chores are fair and evenly distributed amongst the family members. Agree a regular day and time for the chores to be done.

2 For each child and each task, I recommend a three-stage process. First show them how to do it. Second (especially for early adolescents), do it with them the first few times. Then let them do it on their own, praising them when they

do a good job. This strategy takes into account that the adolescent brain is still evolving: being shown how to do the job will reduce the likelihood of your having to clean up afterwards!

3 Be sure to lavish them with praise – not money – when the job is done properly.

4 Make sure they understand that failure to complete the chores will have consequences, which you can negotiate beforehand. Few normal young people are motivated to take out the rubbish, they are motivated to have fun. You can use this to your advantage by withdrawing a privilege (mobile phone, TV, internet or whatever entertains them) if they fail to do the job.

5 Don't nag or shout, or go into broken-record mode (repeating instructions a dozen times). Limit yourself to one, or at the most two, reminders along the lines of 'When in the next 30 minutes would you like to feed the dog/set the table/put away your laundry?' At the second request, say in

a calm but stern voice, 'If you don't do it now, there'll be no [more computer, or whatever] today.' If they don't then go into action, stick by your word and take away the privilege.

Should you pay?

Some parents elect to pay their offspring for work around the house, but I think this is a dangerous strategy. Paying them to do household chores sets up a situation where they are not helping as a natural part of family life or because they want to feel useful – rather, they learn to see it as a financial transaction. This can lead to industrial disputes with drawn-out collective bargaining as they argue that the money isn't worth it and they could get a better paying job elsewhere. And there's no arbitration commission to help you out.

With parents in the 'developed' world being increasingly time-poor, we have much to learn from traditional societies, where it has long been the norm for children to assume such responsibilities.

Growing up in Kenya, I vividly recall watching the local children, from a very early age, engage happily and with observable pride in routine chores under the supervision of adults. The idea of a working childhood is one we all need to embrace, not by stuffing small children down coalmines and up chimneys, but by allowing childhood to flow seamlessly into adult life.

The truth about lying

> 'Matilda told such Dreadful Lies,
> It made one Gasp and Stretch one's Eyes.'
> Hilaire Belloc

Lies range from exaggeration/fibbing, strategic omissions and white lies to out-and-out dishonesty. Lying is not unexpected in teenagers and not necessarily a sign of a deep-seated psycho-pathology. However, a recurring pattern of fibbing should be addressed to find the cause.

Hands up anyone who has never told a fib or a fairytale, or engaged in a little deception? Not exactly a forest of hands raised out there? Of course not – and why would there be? All around us there are relatives, politicians, business leaders and sports stars engaging in the occasional spot of fabrication. Yet despite this, telling lies is a behaviour that many parents find particularly upsetting in their teenagers.

Any self-respecting teenager rapidly figures out that the greatest control they can wield over parents is the control of information. They may lie to protect their privacy or to help them feel separate and autonomous. Generally, the more intrusive or enmeshed parents are, the more likely it is that adolescents will lie by omitting information. Teenagers also may model what they see in adult care-givers and come to believe that lying is acceptable in certain situations, such as not telling a boyfriend or girlfriend the real reasons for breaking up so as not to hurt their feelings.

A recurring pattern of lying to friends could suggest low self-esteem, as experience suggests that young people who are chronic liars often don't feel good about themselves. They may try to improve their status by regaling their peers with stories to keep their attention. If you discover that your adolescent has been lying repeatedly, ask yourself why they might be feeling the need to do so. Are they being ignored? Have they been the butt of jokes or bullying?

A sudden increase in lying can also signal that something's wrong in the family, especially if your child is acting up in other ways, such as stealing or damaging property. Pay particular attention if the victims are other family members: often this is a cry for help. Alternatively, a pattern of compulsive lying may suggest that the young person is depressed and this is their way of obtaining a response and support from peers. In that case, they might benefit from counselling to determine the cause. The Australian Psychological Society (APS) offers a referral service (see the contacts listed at the end of the book).

How to respond to lying

What's a good response if you find that the fruit of your loins has been telling lies? Take some time to have a serious talk about the importance of truthfulness, honesty and trust at home and in the community, and alternatives to lying. Above all, recognise that part of your parenting script is to encourage honesty – as a characteristic, not just a behaviour. When all is said and done, we want our sons and daughters to love the truth, not fear it; and to hate lies, not merely the punishment that lying brings.

- Do understand that all teens tell lies from time to time. Socially acceptable lies form the glue of our society. In a single day, most of us lie a minimum of 25 times.
- But don't ignore lying. The habit, and the problems that lie beneath, will only increase if ignored.

- Don't trigger defensiveness by character assassination. You can reduce the potential power struggle by saying 'I am finding this really hard to believe' rather than 'I know you're lying'. It is harder for them to argue with your beliefs.
- Use consequential learning (see page 31). Set it up with something along the following lines: 'If you choose to lie about what you were doing last night, you choose to lose that privilege for a day.'
- Remember that changing patterns of behaviour can take time, so look for improvements rather than complete elimination. As young people gain self-confidence, the reasons for lying usually diminish.

Anger and arguments

Remember that healthy families fight. There are essentially three ways in which they do so: constructively, where an issue is discussed and resolved; productively (discussed but not resolved); and destructively (with anger, raised voices and sometimes violence). Better out than in, they say, so don't avoid thorny issues – instead, confront them and talk them through.

That said, if you find yourself constantly in conflict with your adolescent, do seek help. You could start with your family doctor, who may refer you to a psychologist, family therapist or family mediation service (see the contacts listed at the end of the book).

Some general dos and don'ts when conflict does occur:

- **Do** state your feelings, but be conscious of your tone of voice, facial expression and body language. Gritting your teeth, squeezing your fists and saying 'I'm not really angry . . . ' sends a mixed message. And do avoid the injured martyr routine.
- **Do** listen attentively and get the facts. Make sure you acknowledge their feelings, experience and point of view.
- **Do** remember that violence is never acceptable.
- **Do** apologise if you lose it – even grown-ups make mistakes sometimes. An apology when we're wrong sets a good example of humility.
- **Don't** overreact – or underreact, for that matter. (Good luck!)
- **Don't** engage in character assassination. In the heat of battle, things are often said that people regret later on. Focus on the behaviour rather than the person: saying 'I love you, it's just your behaviour I can't stand' is a great start.
- **Don't** accuse, insult or talk down to them.

- **Don't** try to control or feel you must always 'win' – it's perfectly okay to lose a few arguments.

Finally, when the heat is off, do rest up for the next encounter – because there will be one!

> '**The best substitute** for experience is being sixteen.'
> Raymond Duncan

The rules of engagement

Following are some suggestions for avoiding conflict, or defusing things once the battle lines are drawn. On issues relating to safety, though – such as drugs, alcohol, sex and sleep – parents should always have the final say.

- **Only argue over things that matter**
  We could light up Australia with the amount of energy that parents expend arguing with teenagers over issues that are

relatively trivial (the time-honoured favourite is carping over an untidy room). The secret of a good relationship with teenagers is to save your powder for the things that really matter. The question to ask yourself is: Does the issue threaten your offspring's health, growth and/or development? The fact is that no one has ever died of an untidy room, so let it go! Fight over issues that matter (curfews, drug use and unsafe sexual practices).

- **Keep calm**

  Yelling achieves nothing, so don't do it. If you carry on like an enraged elephant you are giving your kid buttons to push in the future. Young people learn best through modelling – parents who shout at young people tend to have young people who shout back and become parent-deaf. Why not try whispering? And when you feel like exploding, count to a million or go to the bathroom (or the gym, golf-club, tennis or squash court). If you can't leave the house for some

ARE YOU ALRIGHT MUM?

reason (e.g. you have younger children), try going to your bedroom and screaming quietly into the pillow.

- **Pick the right moment – for both of you**

  When dealing with potentially explosive issues, cool heads are better. Focus on the present situation and what needs to be done. If you can't do this, walk away.

- **Don't assess their behaviour as if they are adults**

  Try to keep in mind that you're the grown-up here: difficult as it can be when provoked, before you open your mouth remember that the last-formed parts of the brain are those responsible for calming down emotions, planning, organising and assessing risk. Ask yourself if you ever made any mistakes or got angry when you were their age. How did your parents respond and how did that make you feel? If it didn't work for you, it won't work for your children. But don't verbalise this: as soon as teenagers hear lectures beginning with words like 'When I was your age' they switch off.

Some lines for defusing conflict
- 'We're getting upset. Let's leave it now and talk later.'
- 'Let me see if I've understood: I think you're saying you feel . . .'
- 'Don't forget I'm on your side.'

- 'Let's finish the argument now, but I want you to have the last word.'

'She had lost the art of conversation but not, unfortunately, the power of speech.'

George Bernard Shaw

Dealing with violent behaviour

Try to remember that violent behaviour often masks feelings and emotions that adolescents don't have the vocabulary to

STEP BACK ... THERE'LL BE SOME FALLOUT

explain. Rather than automatically punishing an adolescent for such behaviour, take a problem-solving approach. This means having a conversation once things have calmed down, to try to understand what lies behind the behaviour, what needs are not being met. Boys, in particular, need time to let us know how they feel about things.

> '. . . Anyone can become angry – that is easy.
> But to be angry with the right person,
> to the right degree, at the right time,
> for the right purpose and in the right way –
> this is not easy.'
>
> Aristotle

What to do if things get out of hand

However difficult it may be in the heat of the moment, it is important to:

- try to stay calm

- give the young person plenty of physical space – angry teens need more room
- name what is going on (e.g. 'I think things are a little out of control – we need help')
- provide hope – tell them that everything is going to be okay
- remove any means by which they can do harm.

Some governments offer a Crisis Assessment service. Different states and territories have different arrangements, so check with your GP for a number to ring in case of an emergency.

When they learn to drive

Motor-vehicle accidents are the leading cause of death for Australian teenagers. Our job is to teach our kids that cars are more than just a means of transport, they can be lethal weapons. It's vital that we give them clear messages about the responsibilities and the dangers of driving.

There is a very good reason why you don't hear many parents waxing lyrical about teaching their own offspring to drive. It's a nightmare: even if you have a warm and cosy relationship with your offspring, sitting in the passenger seat while they learn to drive is something else. The standard advice is to give the job to a professional driving instructor. Once they get their L-plates, though, teens need to gain experience in the company of an adult driver: I think every parent should take advantage of this permit period and give kids as much time as possible behind the wheel.

I'M SURPRISED MUM
DIDN'T WANT TO COME

Handling family breakdown

In Australia some 45 per cent of marriages now end in divorce, with more than 500 000 young people moving between family households each week. This creates the potential for great emotional instability.

There are six golden rules for parents to bear in mind when deciding to separate:

1 Agree with your partner on what's parental business only (e.g. legal and financial arrangements) and what's the

YOUR FATHER AND I ARE SEPARATING

young person's business (e.g. accommodation and access arrangements).

2 Emphasise (repeatedly) to your offspring that they are not responsible for the break-up.

3 Make it clear that there's no chance of a reconciliation.

4 Don't use young people as messengers or pawns in an ongoing war between the partners.

5 Do not use your adolescent as a confidante.

6 Try to maintain as much of your usual routine and structure as possible.

If there are problems, seek help from a qualified family therapist as soon as possible.

A further complication is that the latest statistics suggest nearly one in four families is headed by a single parent. Research also indicates that mental-health problems amongst young people are higher if they live in low-income, single-parent or blended families – and the figure may increase if the parents' separation is acrimonious. This doesn't mean that mental-health problems are inevitable in such situations, but it does mean that the risk is greater. So parents in these circumstances need to be especially alert to the warning signs (see page 125).

Health matters

While compared to the rest of the population adolescents are largely very healthy, some 10–20 per cent of teenagers have chronic illnesses. But the bulk of their health problems lies in the mental-health arena: it is estimated that over 100 000 young Australians suffer from depression, and on average six commit suicide each week in this, the lucky country. This is not the whole picture, however: some 54 per cent use illicit drugs; we have the second highest teenage abortion rate in the western world; and the number of sexually transmitted infections, such as chlamydia in teenage girls, has trebled in the last 10 years.

Disturbingly, a recent study found that 11 per cent of teenage girls had engaged in deliberate self-harm.

These patterns of health-compromising behaviour carry extremely high personal and social costs. Research studies from around the world say that one of the most important preventative factors in the lives of young people is a close relationship with an adult. So it's vital to be informed and to develop appropriate skills and strategies.

Sleep – or the lack of it

The innocent sleep,
The death of each day's life,
sore labour's bath,
balm of hurt minds,
great nature's second course.

William Shakespeare

Sleep is said to occupy one-third of our existence. But as well as television, today's e-generation has computers and the internet (especially on-line games and chat-rooms) to keep them up late at night. An Australian study in 2004 found that 90 per cent of Year 10 students (i.e. 15–16-year–olds) aren't getting enough sleep, and that 15 per cent build up such a substantial sleep debt that they can't even work at school. And as the academic year progresses, this can have a grave impact on their physical and mental wellbeing.

Recent US research suggests that teenagers need as much sleep as small children (about 8.5 to 9.2 hrs) but are generally getting nowhere near that: on week nights the average student gets only about 7.5 hours and one in four students is getting 6.5 hours or less. This research also showed that many teenagers function according to a 'day' of 25–27 hours rather than the normal 24-hour adult cycle. In these teenagers, the melatonin upsurge that helps bring sleep seems to begin only at 11 p.m. or later, which creates problems in the morning because they have trouble waking in time for school.

Of course, it is worth noting that (depending on which sleep expert you speak to) 50–70 per cent of adults don't get enough sleep either, and about 40 per cent are chronically sleep-deprived, though most don't even know it. But the effects of sleeplessness know no age boundaries. During sleepless episodes, immune cells usually used to fight disease are activated and so are more susceptible to outside infections. That's why when we are run-down we have a tendency to get sick. Research suggests too that chronic sleep loss may also impair the body's ability to develop antibodies (the goal of all vaccinations) and that, for example, our response to the flu vaccine is affected by the amount of sleep we had in the days immediately beforehand.

In all walks of life, insufficient sleep has been found to impact on memory, mood and academic performance as well as greatly increasing the risk of accidental injury. The 1989 *Exxon Valdez* oil spill off Alaska, the first space shuttle disaster (*Challenger*) and the Chernobyl nuclear accident have all been attributed to human errors in which sleep deprivation played a role. The Australian insurance company NRMA estimates motorist fatigue to be the third-biggest killer on our roads, currently contributing to one in five motor-vehicle crashes that result in death or serious injury. In Canada, the extra hour of sleep received when clocks are put back at the start of daylight saving has been found to coincide with a fall in the number of road accidents.

Is your teenager sleep-deprived?

It is clear that your adolescent is sleep-deprived if he or she falls asleep at the dinner table or in class, or wakes up tired and grumpy. But there are less obvious signs to look for if you are concerned about their sleep patterns. For example, according to the Australian Sleep Foundation someone who falls asleep in less than five minutes is sleep-deprived. Other clues include:

- poor attention span and motivation, especially for boring tasks requiring sustained concentration
- memory lapses
- decreased initiative, judgement and decision-making
- increased irritability.

. . . and what can you do about it?

There's plenty of sleep-inducing advice available and some of the methods used for babies and adults are equally applicable to adolescents. Most sleep experts agree, for example, that a regular sleep routine (going to bed at about the same time each night) is crucial. Keeping the bed for sleeping – rather than for eating, reading or watching TV – is also suggested, though it must be said that this is less likely to be workable in adolescence.

The beneficial effects of exercise on sleep have also been well documented. A swim, a bike ride or any preferred activity in the afternoon encourages a helpful level of weariness. Exercising just before bedtime is not recommended, however, as it can have quite the opposite effect.

After a hard day at school slaving over a hot Pentium, students often arrive home wound up like a pretzel, anxious and tense. This inevitably makes trying to go to sleep about as easy as nailing jelly to the wall. So encourage them to relax and unwind before trying to get to sleep: a hot bubble bath, relaxing (not head-banging!) music such as Pachelbel's *Canon*, reading a magazine or watching a favourite TV show can be a big help in preparing them for a good night's sleep.

Last but not least, stimulants such as coffee, tea or cola should be avoided for at least two hours before they hit the sack, especially when they are doing final-year exams. The same goes for nicotine, alcohol and other drugs, of course, though hopefully these are not regular features of the household menu. Alcohol in particular is a depressant which may make us drowsy but can seriously disrupt our sleep.

If nothing works . . .

If your adolescent (or you, for that matter) has persistently poor sleep, the good news is that most major hospitals now have sleep units and there are a growing number of privately run sleep units across Australia. For more information contact the Australian Psychological Society's national referral service (see the contacts list at the end of the book).

Sex, love and the whole damned thing

As noted earlier, adolescents are in a transitional phase that involves experimentation and risk-taking, and may lead to hazardous sexual behaviours. There is plenty of evidence to suggest that adolescents are taking more and more unsafe risks around their sexual health, which has become a significant public issue as pregnancy, childbirth and sexually transmitted infection

(STI) are now major contributors to the relative incidence of disease in this age group. Some statistics:

- Teenagers are the most frequent users of emergency contraception at Australian family planning clinics.
- Around 45 per cent of sexually active Australian high-school students do not use condoms consistently.
- Nearly one in three adolescents use condoms without any other form of contraception.

- Adolescents delay seeking prescription contraception for an average of one year after initiating sexual activity.
- Some 50 per cent of adolescent pregnancies occur in the first six months of sexual activity.

It is clear that effective prevention strategies should start well before young people become sexually active. And sex education is the best tool here.

The social angle

Young people are generally exposed to a wide range of attitudes and beliefs in relation to sex and sexuality – from peers, the media, teachers and even politicians. Unfortunately, these often give young people confusing messages. While there is certainly health information out there that emphasises the risks associated with sexual activity, by and large these messages are drowned out by the constant barrage of media images promoting the idea that a sexually active young person is much more attractive, sophisticated and generally 'cool'. Thus the gist of the message received is 'Be sexy, but be good'! So it's important to create an environment where young people can comfortably talk about sexuality. You can counter the confused messages in the following ways:

- Let your child know that romantic and/or sexual feelings are normal during adolescence, starting around mid-adolescence.

YOUR FATHER DIDN'T SEE
MY NAVEL UNTIL AFTER
WE WERE MARRIED

- Remember that adolescents need privacy to explore new feelings and ideas but also need their parents' support and understanding as they negotiate various relationships. So look for ways to show your support: know who their friends or crushes are, and let them know they can ask questions. Be on the lookout for 'teachable moments': if you read, see or hear anything related to sexual health or human relationships, use these to initiate discussion. And when you do so, refer to your own or friends' experiences – don't hesitate to clearly articulate your views and let them know how you feel.
- Find out how many adults they feel they can talk to about sexual issues. Let them know they can discuss anything with you, but that if they feel uncomfortable you'd like to know there is another adult they can talk to.
- No matter how much teenagers 'know' about sex (e.g: through formal sex education or via magazines), they don't really know it. So don't assume you have no wisdom to offer them about relationships.

- Let your offspring know your values about sex if you want to, but make safety the biggest priority (e.g. ensuring they have a Medicare card and access to a youth-friendly doctor or a student counsellor).

The Top 5 adolescent misconceptions about sex

Ongoing discussion is a good way to counter the following fictions, which are alive and well in adolescentland.

1 Everyone's having sex
2 Safe sex equals condom use
3 Everyone's heterosexual
4 You can't get the pill without your parent's permission
5 I'm not at risk of STIs

> 'Telling a teenager the facts of life
> is like giving a fish a bath.'
> Arnold H. Glasow

The family angle

It is worth noting that an adolescent's relationship with the opposite-sex parent seems crucial at this time and tends to set the pattern for relationships with other adults in the future. In addition, if family relationships aren't sound, teenagers tend to seek out or drift into relationships with adults outside the family. And if they start out in a mismatched power relationship, they tend to have that sort of relationship throughout adult life, for we all tend to replicate our early love relationships over and over again.

Sex education: are they getting enough?

Many parents find sex a difficult, often embarrassing, topic, but console themselves that sex education is nowadays part of the school curriculum. Sadly, though, sex education in many schools still focuses mainly on 'plumbing' and on sexually transmitted infection and disease. Few schools cover the human, non-clinical aspects of sex and sexuality – relationships, intimacy,

or alternatives to intercourse such as 'outercourse' (everything that gives sexual pleasure, except penetration).

The paucity of reality-based sex education stems from the rather bizarre and ill-founded view that enlightening our young people will promote earlier sexual activity: in other words, that if you tell them about it they'll do it. This conspiracy of silence is, however, believed by many adolescent health practitioners to be one of the main reasons for our high rates of unplanned pregnancy and STIs among teenagers. And the fact is that in countries with more liberal views, such as Norway, the rates are much lower.

So don't sit back in the hope that your offspring will be having open and frank classroom conversations about sex, for this is rarely the case. The general reticence is compounded by the fact that not only are some teachers (being no different from the rest of the population) embarrassed by the subject but some fear that if they do talk to students about sex this may be misinterpreted as 'grooming' by a paedophile.

It can't be said too often that the great challenge for parents is to create an environment where young people feel free to talk about sex and sexuality. The increased sexual urges children begin to experience at puberty can be confusing and even scary. It is difficult to take these weird feelings and connect them with the boy or girl in class or next door, so it is normal to project them instead onto movie or pop stars, athletes and teachers –

the classic teenage crush, which hopefully is confined to romantic fantasies safely swirling around in their imaginations and dreams. By around middle adolescence they naturally begin to direct their sexual feelings towards their peers.

Most young people can tell you there is huge pressure on them to have sex. Some decide to do so because their friends think sex is cool. Others feel pressured by the person they are dating, and still more say they find it easier to give in and have sex than to try to explain why not. Many adolescent girls get caught up in

the romantic feelings and believe that having sex is the best way they can prove or demonstrate their love for their boyfriend.

'Mum, Dad, I'm gay'

Some parents may be faced with an announcement along these lines. It may test your tolerance, your values, your beliefs, even your self-esteem. Many parents tend to envisage or even map out a future for their son and daughter that involves marriage

and grandchildren. But on hearing that their offspring is gay, these dreams (which often are not articulated) are dashed.

You are likely to have many questions. How/why do people become homosexual? Is this my fault? What can I do? Theories abound about the origins of homosexuality, the most popular one at the moment suggesting that it is hormone levels in the womb, rather than genetic or social traits, that are the determining factor. Whatever the causes, there will always be families with homosexual sons and daughters. The important issue is how we, as parents, deal with it.

It is worth pointing out that many young people question their sexuality from time to time. Being attracted to someone of the same sex is very common and may be nothing more than a temporary crush which they will outgrow. But if your child is gay, how best to approach things?

First of all, get some accurate, up-to-date and reliable information. PFLAG (Parents and Friends of Lesbians and Gays), for example, is a non-profit voluntary support organisation for families of gays and lesbians (see contacts listed at the end of the book).

Perhaps the most important thing is to stay calm. Try to keep your values or beliefs about homosexuality separate from your love for your son or daughter; be open; be sympathetic; and above all offer reassurance, support and understanding. Let them know you love them irrespective of their sexual orientation. Keep in mind that many young people spend months, even years, living in a paralysing state of fear, plagued with uncertainty as to how their families will respond to something over which they have no control. Many are frightened of being kicked out of home and so don't talk about it and often find it hard to access support. Research suggests that homosexual young people are at much greater risk of being bullied, becoming depressed or anxious, feeling suicidal and using illicit drugs.

If you find yourself struggling with the issue, do seek professional advice and support.

What if you only think your child is gay?

If you think your offspring might be gay but you're not sure, don't ask them up-front but rather first let them know that you are comfortable with the issue. If an opportune moment presents itself, ask gently whether they do feel attracted to members of the same sex. You might inquire how long they've felt this way and indicate your willingness and desire to talk further if they so wish.

Drugs

One of the great fears of any parent is that their offspring will try, or worst of all, become dependent on health-threatening and/or illicit drugs. This, of course, is not a new problem. As far back as the 1980s, US First Lady Nancy Reagan championed a War on Drugs campaign that featured as its slogan 'Just Say

No'. The idea was (and still is, in many quarters) that teaching young people creative ways to say no to drugs and simultaneously bolstering their self-esteem will minimise drug use.

Today the media still reports so-called 'experts' who insist that parents can win the war on drugs by simply telling adolescents to say no. Yet this alleged magic bullet has been well and truly discredited: according to an article in the *Journal of Consulting and Clinical Psychology* (August 1999) the 'Just Say No' message not only failed to lower the rate of experimentation with drugs among adolescents, but may also have actually lowered their self-esteem. The findings were abysmal: 20-year-olds who'd been exposed to the message were no less likely to have smoked cigarettes, drunk alcohol or used illicit drugs (marijuana, 'speed', cocaine or heroin). They were also as likely to cave into peer pressure where drug-taking was concerned as were the kids who'd never been exposed to the message. But that wasn't all. Those exposed to the 'Just Say No' message had lower levels of self-esteem 10 years later than those who were never exposed to it. Furthermore another study, performed at the University of Illinois, suggests some high-school students who'd been in 'Just Say No' classes were *more* likely to use drugs than their peers!

Clearly this form of drug education doesn't work. So where did the message come from and why does it persist in the minds of many parents?

'Drugs have taught an entire generation of American kids the metric system.'
P. J. O'Rourke

Just say know
The chief weaknesses of the 'Just Say No' message are its over-simplification of the issue and its panic-level assertions that 'drug

abuse is everywhere'. Young people have never responded well to simplistic generalisations and this sort of anti-drug rhetoric was and still is in danger of turning young people off in droves. But an even greater danger is that making drugs seem more common or 'normal' than they are might push vulnerable kids (who are anxious or depressed, say) towards drugs as a means of belonging or as a form of escape.

As has often been said, the truth is that we lost the war on drugs years ago and Australia-wide research suggests that all young people – yours and mine – will be exposed to illicit and licit drugs relatively early in adolescence.

In my opinion, the ability of school-based education programs to drug-proof our teenagers has been massively oversold. We all need to be much more realistic about what drug education can and cannot do. Harm minimisation (that is, giving young people the skills, knowledge and strategies to handle exposure to drugs) is a more realistic approach. The message we should be giving our adolescents is 'Just Say Know'.

It's not a matter of rejecting formal drug education – our young people need it, especially if it's been properly evaluated and is provided by teachers with appropriate training. But far and away the most important tutors are the adults with whom young people grow up at home.

What can you actually do?

We parents have a central part to play in reducing the likelihood of our children embarking on risky behaviour such as drug-taking, through being good role models and information sources.

As I've already suggested, staying 'connected' with your offspring is perhaps the greatest insurance policy in this regard. Of course, such a bond must be supplemented with accurate and up-to-date information so that young people can make informed choices when exposed to drugs. A great place to start is the Australian Drug Foundation website: www.adf.org.au. (Good luck with your projects!)

Top 5 protective tips

1   As early as possible in adolescence, encourage your offspring to get involved in adult-supervised after-school activities you know they're interested in – art, music, drama, dance, sport. Having an active interest which they enjoy, can do with

friends, and offers the opportunity for them to take safe risks and have some success, allows young people to build self-confidence and makes them less likely to use drugs.

2   Help your kids develop tools they can use to get out of alcohol- or drug-related situations. ('I'd get kicked off the team if I was caught around drugs.' 'I can't, I have a big test tomorrow.' 'No thanks, I've got these infectious boils on my lips at the moment.') Talk about your own experiences and what worked for you!

3   Get to know your kids' friends and their parents. Make contact with the parents to make sure they share your views on alcohol, tobacco and other drugs. If possible, steer your kids away from any friends who regularly use drugs or who are disaffected at school. You could, for example, provide distractions in the form of new and challenging fun activities, and be available to provide transport to the homes of kids you like and trust.

4   Call kids' parents if their home is to be used for a party.

Make sure that the party will be supervised by adults, particularly if those attending are inexperienced and/or known to be risk-takers.

5 Negotiate curfews – and enforce them (see 'Teach them consequential learning' on p. 31).

Depression and other mental-health problems

Australian research suggests that 20–30 per cent of teenagers will develop a mental illness. These include depression, anxiety and eating disorders, all of which can impact upon the young person's ability to get through their day-to-day routine and, worse still, can erode the foundation of their relationships with family, friends and teachers.

Many teens will invest a lot of energy in putting on a good front to fool others, while others will experience unbearable levels of loneliness, anxiety and depression. It is vital that we parents know the difference between normal teenage behaviour and

signs of serious distress. Clinical experience suggests that early diagnosis and prompt treatment are effective but, sadly, a study in 2000 showed that half the young people who experience a mental disorder never receive treatment for it. This is because many young people do not know where to go for help, and parents and teachers do not know what signs to look for.

Almost every parent I know wants their offspring to be happy, healthy and well, to have the capacity to face, overcome and be transformed by adversity – resilient kids who generally feel good about themselves. From time to time, however, parents notice that something is wrong and begin to worry about their teenager's behaviour and have doubts about their ability to cope. Research suggests that one in five young people suffer from emotional problems sufficiently distressing to justify seeking professional help. Their symptoms can range from relatively mild feelings of depression and anxiety to severe distress and dysfunction which can threaten life itself.

What are the warning signs?

- **Frequent sadness, tearfulness, crying**

  Depressed adolescents may often be very tearful or on the brink of tears. They may cry for no apparent reason.

- **Gloomy clothing, writing and music**

  Depressed adolescents may show their sadness and despair by wearing black clothes, writing poetry with morbid themes, or being preoccupied with music with a nihilistic outlook.

- **Poor hygiene and grooming**

  Some may feel that life is simply not worth the effort of looking after themselves or their appearance.

- **Hopelessness**

  They may believe that a negative situation will never change and be constantly pessimistic about their future.

- **Decreased interest in doing 'stuff'**

  Unhappy teens may become apathetic and drop out of clubs, sports and other activities they once enjoyed. Nothing seems fun any more.

- **Persistent boredom and/or low energy**

  A common phrase from depressed teens is that everything is 'boring'. Lack of motivation and lowered energy levels can be reflected in missed classes or truancy, and the resulting drop in marks can be exacerbated by their loss of concentration and slowed thinking.

- **Social isolation**

  Very unhappy young people may withdraw from friends and family. Even those who used to spend a lot of time with friends may now spend most of their time alone and without interests. They may not share their feelings with others, believing that they are alone in the world and no one is listening or cares.

- **Guilt and low self-esteem**

  They may assume blame for negative events or circumstances, feel themselves a failure and have negative views about their competence and self-worth. Seeing themselves as unworthy, they become even more depressed with every supposed rejection or perceived lack of success

- **Increased irritability, anger or hostility**

  One of the key traits in depressed young people is acute
  irritability, where they project their frustration and anger
  onto their family. They may attack others by being critical,
  sarcastic or abusive – they may feel they must reject their
  family before their family rejects them

- **Frequent complaints of physical illnesses, such as
  headaches and stomach-aches**

  Depressed adolescents may have a range of psychosomatic
  symptoms, including lightheadedness or dizziness, nausea
  and back pain. Other common complaints include headaches,
  stomach-aches, vomiting and (for girls) menstrual problems.

- **Disruptive behaviour at school**

  Teens who cause trouble at home or at school may actually
  be depressed but not know it. Because they may not always
  seem sad, parents and teachers may not realise that the
  behaviour is a sign of depression.

- **Poor concentration**
  Bombarded by intrusive and unwanted automatic negative thoughts, the young person may have trouble concentrating on schoolwork, following a conversation, reading a book or even watching television.
- **A major change in eating and/or sleeping patterns**
  Sleep disturbance may show up as all-night television watching, difficulty in getting up for school, or sleeping during the day. They often find it impossible to fall asleep, wake frequently during the night or get stuck in a pattern of early-morning waking. A pattern of comfort eating, more common in girls, may result in weight gain and obesity. Loss of appetite is also common.
- **Talk of or efforts to run away from home**
  Running away is usually a cry for help. This may be the first time that parents realise their child has a problem and needs help.

- **Alcohol and drug abuse**

  Depressed teens may abuse alcohol or other drugs as a way to feel better. Marijuana is a common form of self-medication, but regular use has been found to increase symptoms of depression and anxiety, especially in girls.

- **Self-injury**

  Teens who have difficulty talking about their feelings may show their emotional tension, physical discomfort, pain and low self-esteem with self-injurious behaviours, such as cutting themselves.

Eating disorders

Eating disorders scar the lives of tens of thousands of Australians each year, impacting on three in every 100 Australian females. For all too many it is a death sentence, as up to 20 per cent of sufferers eventually die. Sadly, there is little scientific evidence that conventional treatment works.

The good news is that eating disorders are much easier to prevent than to cure, and we mums and dads are in a great position to help – in the context of the family, not in organised programs. Keep in mind at all times that what you do is a much more powerful message than what you say.

Science is telling us that the genetic factors that determine personality have more influence than previously suspected in the development of eating disorders. Those factors seem to be activated when a vulnerable person begins to restrict their caloric intake in the belief that losing weight will somehow make life happier. At that point parents can start feeling guilty and go into denial. Neither is useful: instead of bemoaning what you did or didn't do, take action and organise an assessment with a mental-health specialist. The sooner treatment is begun, the easier it will be to turn matters around. The longer the symptoms are ignored and the longer you hope it's 'just a phase', the harder the road to recovery will be.

A new approach from Sweden maintains that eating disorders are not a mental illness at all and have nothing to do with family dynamics or physical or emotional abuse, but rather that people slip into a disease cycle as they starve and compulsively exercise. Some 75 per cent of patients trialled in Sweden are going into remission after just 12 months of this treatment. In Australia, up to a quarter of anorexic patients receiving conventional treatments usually relapse within just two years. The Swedish model will, hopefully, soon be available in Australia.

How do you know?
- A marked increase or decrease in weight not related to a medical condition.
- Abnormal eating habits such as severe dieting, preference for strange foods, withdrawn or ritualised behaviour at mealtimes, or secretive bingeing. Related behaviours include self-induced vomiting, periods of fasting, or reliance on laxatives, diet pills or diuretics.

- An intense preoccupation with weight and body image.
- Compulsive or excessive exercising.
- Feelings of isolation, depression or irritability.

Top 5 tips for support

Young people with an eating disorder are often in denial and thus will most likely reject offers of help, preferring to isolate themselves as much as they can. Behaviours such as hiding food rather than consuming it can be very infuriating.

1 Always be ready to listen, try to understand, and always calmly talk things over. Never give up on your offspring.

2 Try not comment on their appearance. A person with an eating disorder will take this to mean they have gained weight and are now 'fat'.

3 Don't blame your child for what is happening. You wouldn't blame them for getting diabetes, asthma or cancer. There's no difference with an eating disorder – it is just another disease.

4 Don't make mealtimes a major drama: they should be as

comfortable and friendly as possible so that your offspring doesn't hate eating. Calmly encourage them to eat snacks.

So what can you do?

In the first instance, you can seek help from your GP. If they know your child, they may be able to suggest the most suitable path. Different states and territories fund counselling services for children and young people up to 18 years of age and their families. These services are provided by child and family specialists including psychologists, psychiatrists, social workers, nurses, occupational therapists and speech pathologists. Your GP or local community health centre should have contact details.

Some thoughts about suicide

One of the most common topics raised with adolescent psychologists is youth suicide. As a parent of two boys, the thought of them committing suicide is simply too terrible to contemplate. All parents want to know the signs that would indicate an adolescent is considering such an act. Before I suggest some, there are a few important points to be made.

While it is cold comfort for the families of the 290 young people aged 15–24 who committed suicide in 2003 (the latest statistics available at the time of writing), the overall youth suicide rate in Australia has actually come down in recent years. In 1997 an average of nine young people ended their lives each week, whereas the figure today is around six. This doesn't mean we can rest on our laurels, but we are clearly headed in the right direction.

> '. . . Suicide, like a great work of art.
> is prepared in the silence of the heart.'
>
> Albert Camus

Why?

Almost everyone has their own pet theory about why young people might kill themselves, ranging from lack of religion, poor parenting, heavy metal music and food colouring to the entire education system. In fact, suicide is best understood as the end point of a journey that can start in many different places.

The problem for those of us looking for a simple preventative strategy is that no single causal factor has been identified. While some young people who take their lives explicitly and repeatedly communicate their intentions to others, many young people never do, instead acting on impulse, sometimes fuelled

by alcohol or drugs, disguising their plans and affording their loved ones no opportunity to intervene. The excruciating fact for so many families is that there is no stereotypical candidate.

It is clear, though, that 70–90 per cent of young people engaging in suicidal behaviour suffer from some form of mental illness, very often depression, which along with other risk factors creates a potentially lethal combination. These risk factors include antisocial behaviour (sometimes known as conduct disorders) and/or alcohol or other drug misuse, a disturbed or unhappy family background, stressful life events (e.g. a relationship break-up or bereavement), and/or knowing people who have committed suicide (especially family members or friends).

Psychological research suggests that the more risk factors present, the more at-risk that person becomes. The complexity stems from the fact that most young people with one or more risk factors present will not attempt suicide and some with minimal risk factors will do so. So what should you be on the lookout for?

As I've said throughout this book, the greatest insurance policy for the wellbeing of young people is to remain emotionally in touch with them. If children and adolescents feel loved within the family, that there is a place for them at home, they may still push the boundaries but their risk-taking will be less hazardous. So rather than just monitoring their behaviour, keep tabs on their emotional life. Look for changes away from a familiar or predictable pattern of behaviour (see page 125).

In addition, depressed teens are at increased risk of committing suicide. If a young person says 'I want to kill myself' or 'I'm going to commit suicide', always take the statement seriously and seek an evaluation from a mental-health professional. It is worth noting that although we often feel uncomfortable talking about death, asking whether he or she is depressed or thinking about suicide can be helpful. Rather than putting thoughts in their head, as some people fear, such a question provides assurance that somebody cares and gives the young person the chance to talk about their problems.

Taking care of yourself

Great parenting is *not* about continual self-sacrifice. All parents have a need for intimacy, companionship, recreation and time alone. Making sure that some of your own needs are met will make you much more able to be patient, consistent and available to your little darling.

QUANTITY TIME

QUALITY TIME

Five ways to keep the stress of parenting at bay

1 **Take your time**
   Most of your everyday activities will take longer when you have one or more teenagers. Give yourself extra time to avoid the feeling of being rushed. When stressed we get tense and anxious, which is contagious. Your children will react better when the pressure is off.

2 **Ask yourself whether an issue is really worth worrying about**
   It's not worth taking a stand over whether plates are left in the sink or put in the dishwasher. Save your energy for issues that really matter to your child's health and your family's wellbeing. Let the little things go by.

3 **Think positive**
   As with your adolescent, when your self-talk is positive you are likely to be calmer and more relaxed. If, for example, you

say to yourself 'I can do this' or 'I'm good at making decisions' you will feel encouraged and less stressed. Negative self-talk such as 'This is terrible' and 'I'm hopeless' will do the opposite and reduce your confidence.

4 Include relaxing activities in your daily routine
Listen to calm music, a relaxation tape or CD, or an audio book, and allow your mind to take a break as well as your body. Your children benefit from a period of quiet time every day and so will you. Do simple relaxation exercises.

Staying calm

It's inevitable that you will sometimes feel as if you're at the end of your tether, or you need to do something to stop you losing your cool with your teenager. These are some practical tips that other parents have found useful to keep tension under control:

- phone a friend or family member
- get some fresh air for a moment
- count to ten, then ask yourself: 'Do I feel calm?' If the answer is no, carry on counting until you can say yes
- laugh out loud. Laughter releases tension
- put on your favourite music
- throw your energy into a big cleaning session
- have a drink of water or make yourself a cup of tea
- think about a loving moment with your teen
- remind yourself of that surge of emotion when your child was born. You could look through a photo album or a diary of your child's birth, for example
- if all else fails, phone a helpline for support.

Conclusion: it's a balancing act

While all young people crave independence and autonomy, great parenting is about finding a balance between giving them privacy and staying connected. Although they will continually seek to push you away, do not allow them to reject you entirely. Keep banging on the door: the more they seek to slam it in your face, the more you have to keep knocking. The key is to keep asking questions, which lets them know that someone cares.

Half a century ago, a guy named Dr Spock told parents, 'You know more than you think you do.' Much of what's in this book is just common sense – we all need a reminder.

Remember, all families have some difficulties . . .

'When I was a boy of fourteen, my father was so ignorant I could hardly stand to have the old man around. But when I got to be twenty-one, I was astonished at how much he had learned in seven years.'

Mark Twain

Useful contacts and links

Australian Drug Foundation – www.adf.org.au
A not-for-profit organisation providing information and a
range of services and programs designed to prevent alcohol
and other drug problems.

Australian Psychological Society – www.psychology.org.au
A psychologist can help by diagnosing and treating problems
such as anxiety, depression or eating disorders, and equipping
young people and their families with the skills needed
to function better. The society offers a referral service to
psychologists in private practice who deal with a particular
problem (phone 1800 333 497).

Child Support Agency – www.csa.gov.au
This site provides access to the latest forms, publications,
brochures, leaflets and other information on CSA issues, in an
immediate, user-friendly way.

Commonwealth Department of Family and Community Services – www.facs.gov.au
This department provides policies, support and assistance for Australian families, communities and individuals (phone 1800 260 402).

Depression Net – www.depressionNet.com.au
Offers advice, support and assistance for sufferers of depression and their families and friends.

DirectLine
A 24-hour counselling, information and referral service for alcohol and drug problems (phone 1800 888 236).

Eating Disorders Foundation – www.edf.org.au
New South Wales site which provides advice and assistance for parents and friends of young people suffering from eating

disorders. Services include practical tips, and links to related organisations in all states and territories.

Family Court of Australia – www.familycourt.gov.au
Great information about the family court, including tips, forms, do-it-yourself kits, and information.

Families, Youth and Community Care Queensland – www.families.qld.gov.au
This site provides families in Queensland with easy access to information to help them meet the challenges of family life.

Family and Children's Services, Western Australia – www.fcs.wa.gov.au
One of the most comprehensive parenting sites in Australia complete with up-to-date information, services and resources to help parents and carers, and kids too.

Fatherhood Foundation – www.fathersonline.org

A charitable, non-profit organisation with a goal to inspire, encourage and educate men to a greater level of excellence as fathers.

Get Your Angries Out – www.members.aol.com/AngriesOut

This was developed to give people alternatives to conflict and violence when they are upset, and help them learn to use their anger in more constructive ways.

Health Insite – www.healthinsite.gov.au

Commonwealth government site providing information about a wide range of health matters including depression, drugs and nutrition. Has comprehensive links to state and territory services.

Kids Help Line (counselling) – www.kidshelp.com.au

Provides free, anonymous and confidential telephone and online counselling services for young people aged 5 to 18 (phone 1800 551 880). Its 'Who Else Can Help' section has the contact details for more than 7000 service providers.

Legal Aid Queensland – www.legalaid.qld.gov.au

Access to legal aid services including duty lawyers, court representation, family and civil law. This site also contains legal information.

Lifeline – www.lifeline.org.au

Longstanding 24-hour telephone counselling service (phone 1300 131 111) which also provides information and referrals for people with mental-health difficulties as well as their families and friends. The website provides a comprehensiv list of Lifeline centres in all states and territories.

Mental Health Information Centre – http://www.mja.com. au/public/mentalhealth/
A valuable resource published by the *Medical Journal of Australia*.

New South Wales Department of Community Services parenting website – www.community.nsw.gov.au
Information on the department's programs, projects and publications about general parenting.

Panic & Anxiety Disorders Assistance – www.pada.org.au
Provides information and resources for people suffering from anxiety disorders or depression, with a view to helping them regain control of their lives. Also offers tips for carers, and links to other organisations in the same field.

Parenting SA – www.parenting.sa.gov.au

Parenting resources and support aimed at helping parents be their best. This site includes parent easy guides, state directory and discussion forum.

Parentlink – http://www.parentlink.act.gov.au

An initiative of the ACT Department of Education, Youth & Family Services. Its confidential telephone information service provides advice, guidance and referrals to anyone who cares for children. The site also has parenting tips and guides, information on community services and events and some great links for parents.

Parentline Victoria – www.parentline.vic.gov.au

A statewide service available to Victorian families with children from birth to 18 years. Professional telephone counsellors provide confidential counselling, information and contact details for community services.

Parent News – www.parent.net

A great source of parent information with articles, news, family facts, homework, tips and resources.

PFLAG – www.pflag.org.au

Based in Victoria and Queensland, Parents and Friends of Lesbians and Gays is a support, information and advocacy group.

Positive Parenting – www.positiveparenting.com

Dedicated to providing resources and information to make parenting rewarding, effective and fun!

Stepfamily Association of South Australia Inc and Stepfamily Australia – www.stepfamily.asn.au

Actively promotes the positive aspects of stepfamily life.

Triple P Parenting – www.triplep.net

The Positive Parenting Program aims to prevent severe behavioural, emotional and developmental problems in children by enhancing the knowledge, skills and confidence of parents.

Index